PRINCEWILL LAGANG

The Role of Humor in Happy Relationships

First published by PRINCEWILL LAGANG 2023

Copyright © 2023 by Princewill Lagang

All rights reserved. No part of this publication may be reproduced, stored or transmitted in any form or by any means, electronic, mechanical, photocopying, recording, scanning, or otherwise without written permission from the publisher. It is illegal to copy this book, post it to a website, or distribute it by any other means without permission.

Princewill Lagang asserts the moral right to be identified as the author of this work.

First edition

This book was professionally typeset on Reedsy.
Find out more at reedsy.com

Contents

1	Introduction	1
2	Exploring the Psychological and Physiological Benefits of...	4
3	Shared Laughter: A Bonding Experience	8
4	The Role of Playfulness	12
5	Diffusing Tension Through Humor	16
6	Communicating Through Comedy	20
7	Playful Teasing and Boundaries	24
8	Shared Humor Styles	28
9	Celebrating Milestones with Levity	32
10	Weathering Life's Challenges with a Smile	36
11	Nurturing a Humorous Environment	39
12	Embracing Joy and Shared Memories	43

1

Introduction

The foundation of any fulfilling and enduring relationship, be it romantic, familial, or platonic, rests on a delicate balance of trust, respect, and emotional connection. These relationships often serve as the bedrock of our lives, offering companionship, support, and a sense of belonging. However, amidst the complexities of human interaction, it's easy to overlook a powerful and underappreciated force that can strengthen, uplift, and deepen these connections: humor.

The Essence of a Happy Relationship

A happy relationship is not a utopia free from challenges; rather, it's a dynamic interplay of emotions, experiences, and shared moments that bring joy, contentment, and resilience. It's about feeling understood, cherished, and accepted for who you are, and reciprocating those feelings. It's the sum of those instances when you look at each other and share a smile, a laugh, or even a knowing glance that transcends words.

The Power of Laughter

Laughter, the universal language of joy, has an uncanny ability to bridge gaps, build bridges, and create bonds. It's a force of nature that transcends cultural, linguistic, and geographical boundaries. Laughter is the spontaneous eruption of happiness, a momentary escape from life's daily grind. When we laugh, we connect not just on an intellectual or emotional level, but on a deeply human one.

The Intersection of Humor and Relationships

At the heart of every meaningful relationship, there's a healthy dose of humor. It's in the playful banter, the shared inside jokes, and the ability to find amusement in life's quirks and absurdities together. Humor acts as a lubricant for communication, making it smoother and more enjoyable. It can defuse tension during disagreements, create lasting memories, and provide a source of comfort in difficult times.

The Connection Between Happiness and Laughter

Happiness and laughter share an inseparable bond. Laughter isn't just a byproduct of happiness; it actively contributes to it. When we laugh, our bodies release endorphins, those magical neurotransmitters responsible for feelings of euphoria. These endorphins not only make us feel good but also reduce stress, alleviate pain, and improve our overall well-being. In essence, laughter has the power to turn ordinary moments into extraordinary ones, infusing happiness into our lives.

Different Forms of Humor

Humor is a multifaceted gem. It comes in various forms, each with

INTRODUCTION

its unique charm and appeal. There's the gentle playfulness of teasing, the observational wit that finds humor in the mundane, the spontaneous outbursts of laughter, and the shared, cherished inside jokes. Individuals have their unique humorous styles, often shaped by their upbringing, culture, and life experiences.

The Plan for the Book

In the chapters that follow, we will delve into the multifaceted world of humor in relationships. We'll explore how humor can be incorporated into various aspects of relationships, from communication to conflict resolution, from celebrations to navigating life's challenges. Through anecdotes, practical tips, and the latest research, we'll uncover the strategies for infusing humor into your relationships to create and sustain happiness.

As we embark on this journey into the world of laughter, remember that humor isn't just a luxury in relationships; it's a vital tool for building lasting connections that weather the test of time. Whether you're seeking to revitalize a long-term partnership, kindle a new romance, or fortify familial ties, the laughter shared along the way will be the glue that holds your happy relationships together.

2

Exploring the Psychological and Physiological Benefits of Laughter

In our quest to understand the pivotal role humor plays in forging lasting and joyful relationships, we must first peel back the layers of laughter's influence on our minds and bodies. Beyond its immediate impact on our emotional state, laughter possesses a profound ability to shape our psychology and physiology, making it a vital ingredient in the recipe for happiness within relationships.

The Psychology of Laughter

Laughter as a Stress Reliever

Picture a tough day at work or a disagreement with a loved one. Now, envision that moment when a joke is cracked, and laughter fills the room. The tension dissipates, and a sense of relief washes over everyone present. Laughter is a potent stress-reliever, and its ability to defuse stressful situations is invaluable in maintaining harmonious relationships.

Laughter as an Emotional Bond

Laughter is the glue that binds hearts. When we share a hearty laugh with someone, we create a unique emotional connection. It signals camaraderie and understanding. It says, "We're in this together." This emotional bond forged through laughter becomes a strong foundation for a happy and resilient relationship.

Laughter and Positive Communication

Effective communication is the lifeblood of any relationship. Laughter can transform communication from mundane to memorable. It lightens the mood, enhances engagement, and makes conversations enjoyable. Couples who weave humor into their conversations tend to experience better understanding and connection.

The Physiology of Laughter

Endorphins: The Elixir of Happiness

Underneath the surface of laughter's psychological magic lies a physiological wonder. When we laugh, our brains release endorphins—our body's natural opioids. These chemicals flood our system, producing feelings of pleasure and reducing physical and emotional pain. Endorphins are nature's mood elevators, and laughter is the switch that activates them.

Laughter's Immune-Boosting Effects

Laughter isn't just a mood enhancer; it's also a defender of health. Studies have shown that laughter can bolster the immune system by increasing the production of antibodies and activating immune cells. In other words, laughter doesn't just make you feel better; it helps you stay healthier too.

Laughter's Physical Release

Ever laughed so hard that your sides hurt, or tears streamed down your face? That's the physical aspect of laughter. It's a workout for your diaphragm, chest, abdominal, and facial muscles. Just as physical exercise is good for your body, so is laughter. It gets the blood flowing, burns calories, and leaves you with a sense of relaxation.

Laughter as a Relationship Asset

Laughter isn't just a fleeting emotion; it's a tool that, when wielded skillfully, can enrich relationships. Its power lies in its ability to simultaneously soothe and invigorate our minds and bodies, making it a vital asset in navigating the ups and downs of life together.

Laughter's Role in Conflict Resolution

When conflicts arise, laughter can act as a mediator. It can break the ice and defuse tension. We'll explore in later chapters how humor can be used to resolve disputes without escalating them, turning disagreements into opportunities for growth.

Laughter's Contribution to Emotional Intimacy

Laughter opens the door to vulnerability. When we laugh together, we lower our guards, revealing our authentic selves. In this state of emotional intimacy, bonds deepen, and relationships flourish.

The Journey Ahead

As we unravel the layers of humor's influence on relationships, remember that laughter isn't just a sound or a reaction; it's a dynamic force that molds our psychology and physiology. It's a tool we can employ to build happier, healthier, and more resilient relationships. In the chapters to come, we will delve into practical ways to infuse humor into your relationships, exploring its multifaceted role in communication, bonding, and resilience. By understanding the science of laughter and its profound effects, we equip ourselves to create relationships brimming with joy and connection.

3

Shared Laughter: A Bonding Experience

Laughter has a remarkable power to create connections, and there's no stronger bond than the one formed through shared laughter. In this chapter, we'll explore how humor creates a sense of unity within relationships, making them more resilient, intimate, and enduring. From inside jokes to humorous memories, the threads of shared laughter weave a tapestry of togetherness in our relationships.

The Significance of Shared Laughter

Creating a Sense of Belonging

Shared laughter is a universal language that signifies belonging. When two people laugh together, they acknowledge their shared experiences, values, and perspectives. It's like having a secret code that only the two of you understand, creating a unique connection.

Strengthening Emotional Intimacy

Humor plays a vital role in emotional intimacy. When couples laugh together, they reveal their genuine selves, free from pretenses or defenses. This authenticity deepens the emotional bond, fostering trust, understanding, and vulnerability.

Forging Lasting Memories

Some of the most cherished memories in relationships are those adorned with laughter. Whether it's the time you both laughed uncontrollably at a silly mishap or the inside joke you've carried through the years, these moments create lasting imprints on your shared history.

Inside Jokes: The Secret Language of Love

Inside jokes are like treasure chests of shared laughter. They are humorous references that only you and your partner understand, creating a world of your own. Inside jokes build a unique connection, enhancing the sense of togetherness.

Creating Inside Jokes

Inside jokes often emerge organically from shared experiences. It could be a funny incident during a vacation, a memorable misunderstanding, or a recurring humorous situation. These jokes become a delightful reminder of your adventures together.

The Evolution of Inside Jokes

Inside jokes evolve and deepen over time. What starts as a simple phrase or reference can develop into a rich tapestry of shared experiences and humor. These jokes strengthen the sense of connection as they accumulate.

Inside Jokes Beyond Romance

Inside jokes aren't exclusive to romantic relationships. They can be found in friendships, familial bonds, and even among colleagues. These humorous connections enhance any type of relationship, making them more enjoyable and meaningful.

Humorous Memories: The Glue of Relationships

Memories tinged with laughter hold a special place in our hearts. Whether it's recalling the time you both got lost on a road trip or the hilarious mishaps at a family gathering, these memories become cherished stories in your relationship.

Creating Humorous Memories

Humorous memories are often born out of spontaneity. They arise when we let go of inhibitions and embrace the whimsical nature of life. By being open to laughter in everyday experiences, you increase the chances of creating these precious moments.

The Impact of Humorous Memories

Humorous memories serve as a source of joy and comfort during difficult times. They remind us of the lighter side of life, offering a respite from stress and challenges. Sharing these memories reinforces your bond and reminds you of your capacity to find joy together.

Conclusion

In shared laughter, we discover the magic of togetherness. Inside jokes and humorous memories become the building blocks of enduring relationships. They are the intimate, unique stories that only you and your loved one share.

SHARED LAUGHTER: A BONDING EXPERIENCE

As we continue this journey into the world of humor and relationships, remember that shared laughter is the glue that binds hearts, making your connection stronger and more resilient with each passing moment.

4

The Role of Playfulness

In the world of relationships, the ability to infuse playfulness is like a secret elixir. Playfulness transcends the ordinary and keeps the spark alive. In this chapter, we'll delve into the significance of playfulness in romantic relationships, exploring how it can breathe life into your connection and nurture a sense of joy that endures.

The Significance of Playfulness

Creating an Atmosphere of Lightness

Playfulness is the art of infusing lightness into your relationship. It's about letting go of rigid expectations and embracing spontaneity. It's the ability to see the world with a childlike wonder, even when adulthood demands seriousness.

Nurturing Connection

Playfulness fosters connection. When you play together, you bond more deeply. It creates shared experiences that become treasured memories. Playful interactions are often remembered long after the laughter has faded.

Rekindling Passion

Playfulness is an aphrodisiac for romance. It adds an element of excitement and novelty to your relationship. Playful teasing, flirty banter, and fun surprises can reignite the flames of passion.

The Role of Playful Activities

Infusing Daily Life with Playfulness

Playfulness doesn't require grand gestures; it can be found in the small, everyday moments. It's in the impromptu dance in the living room, the playful snowball fight, or the shared dessert that becomes a delightful food fight.

Playful Activities That Nurture Connection

1. Exploring Together: Whether it's hiking in nature, strolling through an art gallery, or trying out a new hobby, exploring new experiences together can be an exciting way to infuse playfulness into your relationship.

2. Games and Challenges: Board games, card games, and friendly competitions can bring out the playful spirit. Engaging in challenges, be it a cooking contest or a scavenger hunt, can add a touch of excitement.

3. Travel Adventures: Traveling together opens the door to playful exploration. It's a chance to step out of your routine and discover new places and

cultures.

4. Creative Pursuits: Engaging in creative activities, whether it's painting, writing, or crafting, encourages playfulness. It's about expressing yourselves in unique and imaginative ways.

The Importance of Spontaneity

Spontaneity is the lifeblood of playfulness. It's the willingness to let go of plans and embrace the unexpected. Spontaneous acts of playfulness, like a surprise date night or an unplanned picnic, can breathe freshness into your relationship.

The Playful Side of Physical Touch

Physical touch, beyond its sensual aspect, can also be playful. Playful tickling, cuddling, and physical games like wrestling can evoke laughter and strengthen your connection.

Laughter as a Shared Language

Laughter is the language of playfulness. It transcends words and communicates joy, acceptance, and love. The more you laugh together, the more you speak this shared language, deepening your bond.

Balancing Playfulness and Responsibility

While playfulness is essential, it's crucial to strike a balance with the responsibilities of life. Open communication about your needs for both play and responsibility ensures that neither aspect of your relationship is neglected.

Conclusion

THE ROLE OF PLAYFULNESS

Playfulness is the thread that stitches joy into the fabric of your relationship. It's the element that transforms ordinary moments into extraordinary ones. As you journey through life together, remember to play, laugh, and let the spirit of playfulness infuse your connection with a sense of adventure and delight. In the chapters ahead, we'll explore more ways to nurture this spirit, ensuring that your relationship remains a playground of love and laughter.

5

Diffusing Tension Through Humor

Conflict is an inevitable part of any relationship, but the way we handle it can make all the difference. In this chapter, we'll explore the art of diffusing tension through humor, examining how laughter can be a powerful tool for turning conflicts into opportunities for growth and deeper connection.

The Nature of Conflict in Relationships

The Inevitability of Disagreements

In any relationship, whether romantic, familial, or platonic, disagreements are bound to arise. It's important to acknowledge that conflict isn't inherently negative; it's a natural consequence of differing perspectives and needs.

The Impact of Unresolved Conflict

Unresolved conflicts can fester, creating emotional distance and eroding the foundation of trust. On the other hand, addressing conflict constructively can lead to greater understanding and emotional intimacy.

The Role of Humor in Conflict Resolution

Lightening the Mood

Humor has a remarkable ability to lighten the mood. When tensions run high, a well-timed joke or a playful comment can act as a pressure valve, releasing pent-up emotions and allowing both parties to relax.

Defusing Defensiveness

Conflict often triggers defensiveness, making productive communication challenging. Humor can disarm defensiveness by creating a non-threatening atmosphere. It encourages open dialogue by reducing the fear of judgment or rejection.

Creating Perspective

Humor provides a fresh perspective. It can help you see the situation from a different angle, challenging your assumptions and entrenched viewpoints. This shift in perspective can pave the way for compromise and resolution.

Using Humor Sensitively and Respectfully

Know Your Audience

Not all humor is appropriate in every situation. It's essential to be sensitive to your partner's mood and boundaries. What's funny in one moment may not be in another. Gauge your partner's receptiveness to humor during conflicts.

Avoiding Hurtful Humor

While humor can be a powerful tool, it should never be used to demean, belittle, or hurt your partner. Sarcasm, mockery, and personal attacks have no place in conflict resolution. Healthy humor should be inclusive and light-hearted.

The Timing of Humor

Timing is crucial when using humor in conflict resolution. Avoid making jokes when your partner is highly emotional or upset. Instead, use humor when tensions have slightly eased, and both of you are open to a more relaxed conversation.

Examples of Humor in Conflict Resolution

Playful Teasing

Gently teasing your partner during a disagreement can break the tension. For example, if you're debating where to go for dinner, a playful comment like, "Well, we could always flip a coin or have a staring contest" can inject humor into the situation.

Self-Deprecating Humor

Self-deprecating humor, where you playfully make fun of yourself, can lighten the mood. If you've made a mistake, acknowledging it with humor can reduce defensiveness. For instance, saying, "I guess my superhero power isn't decision-making" adds a touch of levity.

The Power of Shared Laughter

Sharing a humorous observation about the situation can create a sense of camaraderie. For instance, if you're both lost while driving, commenting, "We make the best explorers, don't we?" can draw a smile and ease frustration.

Conclusion

Conflict doesn't have to be a battlefield; it can be a playground for growth and understanding. By infusing humor into your conflict resolution toolkit, you transform disagreements into opportunities to deepen your connection. In the chapters to come, we'll continue to explore how humor can enhance various aspects of your relationship, from communication to celebration, ensuring that your journey together is one filled with laughter, love, and growth.

6

Communicating Through Comedy

Communication is the lifeblood of any relationship. It's the bridge that connects hearts and minds. In this chapter, we'll explore the unique way humor facilitates communication, enabling couples to navigate complex emotions, convey love, and gain deeper understanding through light-hearted conversations.

The Language of Laughter

Non-Verbal Communication

Humor often transcends words. It's expressed through smiles, laughter, and playful gestures. These non-verbal cues are powerful communicators of affection, joy, and connection.

Conveying Love and Affection

COMMUNICATING THROUGH COMEDY

Humor provides a playful avenue for expressing love. A well-timed joke, a funny pet name, or a shared smile all convey affection. These gestures remind your partner that you cherish and enjoy their company.

Navigating Complex Emotions

Lightening Heavy Conversations

Difficult conversations often carry a heavy emotional weight. Humor can serve as a counterbalance, lightening the emotional load and making it easier to discuss challenging topics.

Addressing Sensitive Issues

Humor can be used to address sensitive issues indirectly. For example, if discussing finances is a touchy subject, using humor can break the ice. Saying something like, "Our budget meeting is ready for action!" can make a daunting discussion more approachable.

Enhancing Engagement

Active Listening Through Humor

Engaging in humorous conversations requires active listening. You need to tune in to your partner's cues and respond with witty remarks or playful banter. This active engagement fosters attentiveness and empathy.

The Joy of Shared Interests

Couples often have shared interests and hobbies that form the basis of their humor. Whether it's a mutual love for a particular TV show, a hobby, or a quirky fascination, these shared interests provide a treasure trove of inside jokes and playful references.

Creating Light-Hearted Rituals

Cultivating Connection Through Traditions

Creating light-hearted rituals within your relationship enhances communication. These traditions, whether it's a daily joke, a weekly movie night, or a monthly game night, provide structure for enjoyable, regular communication.

The Power of Humorous Rituals

Rituals add predictability and comfort to a relationship. Humorous rituals, in particular, create anticipation and excitement. They reinforce the idea that your relationship is a source of joy and laughter.

Laughter as a Problem-Solver

Harnessing Creativity Through Humor

When faced with challenges, humor can inspire creative problem-solving. A playful, out-of-the-box approach can lead to innovative solutions that might not have surfaced in a more serious conversation.

Resolving Disagreements Amicably

Humor can be used to diffuse disagreements and find common ground. Playful negotiation and compromise can turn conflicts into opportunities for cooperation rather than contention.

Conclusion

Communication is the bridge that connects hearts, and humor is the hand that extends an invitation to cross it. By embracing humor as a means of communication, you enrich your connection, making conversations more engaging, light-hearted, and memorable. In the upcoming chapters, we'll continue to explore how humor enhances different facets of relationships, from addressing boundaries to celebrating milestones, ensuring that your journey together is one marked by laughter and understanding.

7

Playful Teasing and Boundaries

Teasing is a double-edged sword in relationships. When done with affection and sensitivity, it fosters connection and adds a layer of playfulness to your bond. However, it can quickly become hurtful if boundaries are disregarded. In this chapter, we'll explore the balance between playful teasing and respecting boundaries, ensuring that humor in your relationship remains a source of joy rather than pain.

The Dynamics of Playful Teasing

Affectionate Ribbing

Playful teasing often involves light-hearted, affectionate ribbing. It's a way of expressing love and comfort in a relationship. For instance, making fun of your partner's quirky habits or endearing quirks can create laughter and connection.

Shared Inside Jokes

Playful teasing often leads to shared inside jokes, creating a sense of unity. These jokes are like secret language between partners, further deepening your connection.

The Fine Line Between Teasing and Harm

Teasing can quickly cross into hurtful territory if it becomes personal, critical, or offensive. It's crucial to be aware of your partner's sensitivities and establish boundaries to ensure that teasing remains playful.

The Importance of Boundaries

Understanding Your Partner's Limits

Each person has their unique boundaries when it comes to teasing. Some may be comfortable with light teasing about certain topics, while others may have more sensitive areas. Open communication is key to understanding and respecting these limits.

Creating a Safe Space

In a healthy relationship, boundaries create a safe space for both partners to be themselves without fear of ridicule or judgment. This safe space is essential for building trust and emotional intimacy.

Using Teasing to Strengthen Connection

Enhancing Communication

Playful teasing can enhance communication by creating a relaxed, open atmosphere. It often paves the way for more honest conversations and self-disclosure.

Defusing Tension

Teasing can be a valuable tool for diffusing tension during disagreements. A well-timed, light-hearted comment can break the ice and redirect the conversation toward resolution.

Balancing Teasing with Affection

Affirming Love and Affection

It's essential to balance teasing with expressions of love and affection. Remind your partner that teasing is a sign of your comfort and closeness, not a form of criticism.

Reinforcing Positive Qualities

Playful teasing should also highlight your partner's positive qualities. Compliments, even in jest, can boost self-esteem and deepen your bond.

The Role of Mutual Consent

Expressing Boundaries

Both partners should feel comfortable expressing their boundaries regarding teasing. An open and non-judgmental conversation can clarify what's off-limits and what's fair game.

Consent as a Continuous Process

Consent isn't a one-time agreement; it's an ongoing process. It's essential to check in with your partner regularly to ensure that boundaries are respected and that teasing remains enjoyable for both.

Conclusion

Playful teasing can be a delightful facet of a relationship when approached with sensitivity and respect. It's a way of celebrating each other's quirks and endearing qualities. In the upcoming chapters, we'll continue to explore how humor enhances different aspects of relationships, from understanding shared humor styles to celebrating milestones. By mastering the art of playful teasing within your boundaries, you can ensure that humor remains a source of joy, laughter, and connection in your relationship.

8

Shared Humor Styles

Every person has a unique sense of humor shaped by their experiences, culture, and personality. Understanding and appreciating your partner's humor style can be instrumental in deepening your connection. In this chapter, we'll explore different humor styles and preferences in relationships, and how embracing these differences can enhance your bond.

The Diversity of Humor Styles

The Role of Upbringing

Our childhood experiences play a significant role in shaping our sense of humor. The types of humor we were exposed to, whether it's slapstick comedy or dry wit, influence our preferences.

Cultural Influences

Cultural background also impacts humor. What's considered funny in one culture might not translate to another. Being aware of these cultural nuances is crucial in understanding your partner's humor.

The Types of Humor Styles

Slapstick and Physical Comedy

Some people enjoy humor that's rooted in physicality, like slapstick comedy. They appreciate pratfalls, exaggerated expressions, and comedic mishaps.

Wit and Wordplay

Others gravitate toward witty humor, reveling in clever wordplay, puns, and intellectual jokes. For them, humor is a form of mental gymnastics.

Observational Humor

Observational humor involves finding the funny side of everyday situations. It's about noticing the quirks and absurdities of life and sharing them with a humorous twist.

Sarcasm and Irony

Sarcasm and irony involve saying one thing but meaning another, often with a humorous or satirical intent. Some people thrive on this form of humor, finding delight in its subversive nature.

Self-Deprecating Humor

Self-deprecating humor involves making fun of oneself. It's a way of poking fun at your own quirks and insecurities, often endearing you to others.

Understanding Your Partner's Humor Style

Active Listening

To understand your partner's humor style, pay attention to what makes them laugh. Take note of the types of jokes or comedy shows they enjoy.

Open Communication

Discuss your humor preferences openly. Share what you find funny and ask your partner to do the same. This conversation can deepen your understanding of each other's humor.

Embracing Differences

The Beauty of Diversity

Embracing different humor styles in a relationship can be incredibly enriching. It brings variety and novelty to your interactions, keeping things fresh and exciting.

Respecting Boundaries

While embracing diversity is essential, it's equally vital to respect your partner's boundaries. If a particular form of humor makes them uncomfortable, be mindful not to push their limits.

Sharing Laughter

Creating Moments of Shared Laughter

Share humor by watching comedy shows, attending stand-up performances, or simply swapping jokes. The act of sharing laughter strengthens your connection.

Incorporating Humor into Everyday Life

Infuse humor into your daily routines. Leave funny notes, share amusing anecdotes, or playfully tease each other. This constant injection of humor keeps your bond vibrant.

Conclusion

In the tapestry of a relationship, humor is a thread woven with diverse shades and textures. Embracing your partner's unique humor style is an opportunity to celebrate their individuality and deepen your connection. In the chapters ahead, we'll explore more ways to infuse humor into your relationship, from celebrating milestones to navigating life's challenges. By understanding and appreciating the diversity of humor styles, you can create a richer, more laughter-filled partnership.

9

Celebrating Milestones with Levity

Milestones in a relationship mark moments of growth, commitment, and shared history. While these occasions often come with a sense of seriousness, they can be enriched by infusing humor. In this chapter, we'll explore the role of humor in celebrating milestones and how it can enhance these memorable moments.

The Significance of Relationship Milestones

Markers of Progress

Relationship milestones signify progress and evolution. They're a testament to your journey together, from the initial spark to the deepening of your connection.

Opportunities for Reflection

Milestones provide opportunities to reflect on your relationship's strengths, challenges, and the love you've cultivated. They encourage introspection and gratitude.

The Power of Humor in Celebrations

Lightening the Atmosphere

Humor can infuse celebrations with an element of lightness. It takes the edge off formal or serious occasions, making them more enjoyable and less intimidating.

Creating Lasting Memories

Incorporating humor into milestone celebrations can lead to memorable moments that you'll cherish for years to come. These humorous memories become a part of your shared history.

Humor in Relationship Milestones

Anniversaries

Anniversaries are occasions for reflection and celebration. In addition to heartfelt expressions of love, consider adding a touch of humor. Share amusing anecdotes from your journey together, recount funny mishaps, or exchange humorous vows for a renewal ceremony.

Engagements and Weddings

While wedding ceremonies are often formal affairs, humor can be skillfully woven into vows, speeches, or even the wedding program. A well-timed joke or a playful ritual can add levity without diminishing the significance of the day.

Moving In Together

The decision to move in together is a significant milestone. Celebrate it by embracing the humorous aspects of cohabitation, from adjusting to each other's habits to navigating shared responsibilities.

Big Life Transitions

Major life transitions, like purchasing a home, having children, or retiring, can be accompanied by stress. Humor can be a powerful tool to ease tension during these transitions, turning them into moments of joy.

Customized Humor

Tailor your humor to the milestone and your partner's preferences. Some may appreciate a heartfelt letter with a touch of humor, while others might enjoy a creative, funny gift.

Balancing Humor and Seriousness

While humor is valuable, it's important to strike a balance. Not all milestones are suited for humor, and it's essential to gauge the tone of the occasion and your partner's feelings.

Creating Traditions

Establishing humorous traditions around milestones can make them even more special. Whether it's a silly anniversary tradition or a playful ritual during moving day, these traditions reinforce the importance of humor in your relationship.

Conclusion

Celebrating milestones is a way of acknowledging the journey you've undertaken together. By infusing these moments with humor, you not only create joyful memories but also reinforce the idea that your relationship is a source of laughter and happiness. In the following chapters, we'll explore more ways to nurture humor in your relationship, from weathering life's challenges to infusing daily life with laughter. Through humor, you can enhance your connection and build a relationship that's resilient and brimming with joy.

10

Weathering Life's Challenges with a Smile

Life is a journey filled with both joys and trials. In a relationship, how you face challenges together can define the strength of your bond. In this chapter, we'll explore how humor can be a source of resilience during difficult times, providing strategies for finding silver linings and maintaining positivity.

The Role of Humor in Resilience

Fostering Positivity

Humor can act as a beacon of positivity during challenging moments. It helps you see the brighter side of a situation and maintain a hopeful outlook.

Building Resilience

Resilience is the ability to bounce back from adversity. Humor not only helps you endure difficult times but also strengthens your capacity to overcome future challenges.

Finding Silver Linings

The Art of Reframing

Humor often involves reframing situations in a lighthearted way. Instead of dwelling on the negative, look for opportunities to find humor in adversity.

Coping with Stress

Stress is a natural response to challenges, but excessive stress can harm relationships. Humor acts as a stress reliever, reducing tension and promoting emotional well-being.

Strategies for Maintaining Positivity

Shared Laughter Rituals

Create rituals that encourage shared laughter, even during tough times. It could be watching a favorite comedy show together or playing a silly game to lighten the mood.

Humorous Perspective Shifting

Encourage each other to view challenges through a humorous lens. Ask questions like, "How will we look back on this in a year and laugh?" to foster a sense of perspective.

The Power of Playfulness

Engage in playful activities that provide a respite from stress. Dancing, playing board games, or engaging in creative hobbies can be therapeutic.

Supporting Each Other

Emotional Support

Use humor as a tool to support each other emotionally. Sometimes, a simple joke or a shared laugh can convey empathy and understanding more effectively than words.

Avoiding Hurtful Humor

During challenging times, emotions can run high. Be cautious about using humor that might unintentionally hurt or offend your partner. Instead, focus on uplifting and positive humor.

Humor in Coping with Loss

Loss and grief are part of life. Humor can play a role in the healing process, allowing you to remember and celebrate the life of a loved one with fondness rather than solely with sadness.

Conclusion

Life's challenges are inevitable, but your response to them can strengthen your relationship. Humor is a valuable tool for navigating adversity with grace and resilience. By finding silver linings, maintaining positivity, and supporting each other with humor, you can weather life's storms together and emerge even stronger. In the chapters to come, we'll continue to explore how humor enhances different aspects of your relationship, from infusing daily life with laughter to creating lasting memories filled with joy.

11

Nurturing a Humorous Environment

In the hustle and bustle of daily life, it's easy to forget the importance of laughter and humor in a relationship. In this chapter, we'll explore ways to infuse humor into daily life as a couple, creating an environment that encourages laughter, joy, and a deeper connection.

The Necessity of Daily Humor

Daily Stressors

Life is filled with stressors, from work pressures to household responsibilities. Daily humor acts as a soothing balm, relieving stress and creating moments of respite.

Building Resilience

A humorous environment fosters resilience. When you face difficulties with humor, you're better equipped to overcome challenges together.

Creating Opportunities for Laughter

Morning Rituals

Start the day with humor. Share funny anecdotes, silly jokes, or amusing stories during breakfast. It sets a positive tone for the day.

Playful Communication

Infuse your everyday conversations with playfulness. Use humorous nicknames, witty banter, or amusing pet names when addressing each other.

Shared Activities

Engage in activities that naturally bring laughter. This could be cooking together, playing with pets, or watching a comedy show.

Spontaneous Acts of Humor

Surprise your partner with spontaneous acts of humor. Leave funny notes, send humorous texts, or prepare a surprise that's sure to make them smile.

Humor in Problem-Solving

Use humor to tackle problems together. When faced with challenges, ask each other, "How can we make this situation more humorous?" This approach can help you find creative solutions and maintain a positive outlook.

Fostering an Environment of Acceptance

Accepting Imperfections

Humor often stems from embracing imperfections and quirks. It's a reminder that your partner's idiosyncrasies are what make them unique and lovable.

Laughing at Yourself

Encourage each other to laugh at yourselves. Self-deprecating humor can be endearing and creates a sense of vulnerability and authenticity.

Shared Laughter Rituals

Create daily or weekly rituals centered around humor. It could be a Friday night comedy movie night, a "joke of the day" text, or a playful competition like who can come up with the silliest joke.

The Importance of Adaptability

Flexibility and adaptability are crucial in creating a humorous environment. Be open to trying new things, exploring different types of humor, and adjusting your approach based on your partner's preferences.

Balancing Humor and Seriousness

While humor is vital, balance is key. There will be moments that require serious conversations and emotional support. It's important to gauge the appropriate tone for each situation.

Conclusion

Nurturing a humorous environment is like tending to a garden of laughter in your relationship. It requires daily care and attention, but the rewards are boundless. By infusing daily life with humor, you create a space where joy, laughter, and a deeper connection flourish. In the final chapter, we'll reflect on the role of humor in creating lasting memories and summarize key takeaways to help you cultivate humor in your relationship.

12

Embracing Joy and Shared Memories

As we conclude our journey through the role of humor in happy relationships, we reflect on the profound impact that laughter and humor have on creating lasting memories. In this final chapter, we'll explore the role of humor in building a treasure trove of shared memories, summarize key takeaways, and encourage you to continue cultivating humor in your relationship.

The Legacy of Shared Memories

Building a Story Together

Your relationship is a story in the making, and humor is one of its most colorful chapters. The memories you create together are the foundation of your shared history.

Laughter as Glue

Laughter is the glue that binds your memories. It enhances their vividness and ensures they endure, even as time passes.

Humorous Memories

Inside Jokes and Shared References

Inside jokes and shared humorous references become part of your relationship's unique language. They strengthen your connection and provide moments of laughter even in mundane situations.

Anniversary of Laughter

Celebrate your "anniversary of laughter" by revisiting the moments that made you laugh the hardest. Reminiscing about these moments rekindles the joy they brought.

The Importance of Playfulness in the Mundane

Transforming Everyday Life

Humor has the magical ability to transform ordinary moments into extraordinary ones. It's not just about the grand adventures but also the playful interactions during daily life.

Falling in Love Again and Again

Cultivating humor ensures that you continue to fall in love with your partner, not just once, but over and over again. Each playful moment is a reminder of what makes your relationship special.

Reflections on Your Journey

Rediscovering Joy in the Mundane

Through humor, you can rediscover the joy in everyday life. Whether it's laughing at a kitchen mishap or sharing a knowing glance during a boring meeting, humor adds sparkle to the ordinary.

Laughter as a Bonding Ritual

Your shared laughter rituals, like movie nights, silly games, or spontaneous dance-offs, become cherished bonding rituals that strengthen your connection.

Key Takeaways

1. Humor Is a Language: Understand that humor is a unique language in your relationship. Embrace the diversity of humor styles.

2. Balance Is Key: Find a balance between humor and seriousness. Humor should enhance your connection, not diminish it.

3. Respect Boundaries: Always respect each other's boundaries when using humor. What's funny to one person may not be to another.

4. Shared Memories: Create a treasure trove of humorous memories. Inside jokes and shared references add depth to your bond.

5. Infuse Daily Life with Humor: Make humor a part of your daily routine. Create shared rituals that encourage laughter.

6. Resilience through Humor: Use humor as a tool to weather life's challenges. It fosters resilience and maintains positivity.

7. Celebrate Milestones with Levity: Embrace humor during significant

milestones to create memorable and joyful moments.

Conclusion

As you close this chapter on the role of humor in happy relationships, remember that your relationship is a journey filled with laughter, joy, and shared memories. Humor is the thread that stitches these moments together, creating a tapestry of love and connection. Embrace the joy of laughter, and let humor be your compass as you navigate the beautiful adventure of your relationship. Continue to cultivate humor, for it is the key to keeping your connection vibrant, enduring, and endlessly joyful.

www.ingramcontent.com/pod-product-compliance
Lightning Source LLC
LaVergne TN
LVHW012129070526
838202LV00056B/5932